What is the name of the college being considered? Location? Public or private? Website? Instagram? Facebook? Twitter?

What are my selection criteria? (Example: school size, costs, location) What is important in making my decision? My priorities?

How do I feel about the reputation of the school? Nationally known? Top in region? Ranking for my major?

What majors are available that I am interested in?

What is the placement rate for my major? What type of organizations are hiring?

How far away from home is this campus? Is the commute via car, train, bus, plane? Is this acceptable for me?

What is the average SAT/ACT score? Does my academic background fit?

What is the academic calendar? When does school start? end? Any fall breaks or long weekends? Holidays?

What are the costs for tuition? Room and board?
Books and supplies?

What scholarships are available? Student loans? Work study?

Are part time jobs available on campus? Off campus? What are average hourly earning rates for students?

Is the college experiencing a budget deficit or surplus? Up-tick or down-tick in number of students? Large donations?

When did the most recent building renovation occur? Are there new facilities under construction? Building conditions?

How many students attend this college? Does it feel cramped or spacious?

How was the administrative staff? Did I feel welcome?

Is the college focused more on academics or more on developing you as a whole person? How can you determine?

What are methods for getting around campus?
Walk? Bike? Bus? Can a freshman have a car? Do
I need a car?

Did I feel safe on campus? Are there well lighted areas?

What is the surrounding community/area like?
High or low crime? Parks nearby? Urban area?
Museums?

How is the campus food? Are there a variety of food plans? Cafeteria? Food court?

What is the percentage of students from out-of-state? Anyone from my high school? Where are the students from?

How was the student center? Book store?
Common study areas?

How do I like the dorms? Did I see some cool dorm ideas? How many students to a room/suite? Visitation policy?

How is the technology on campus? WiFi everywhere? WiFi in dorms?

Did I meet any teachers? How did they make me feel?

Did I meet anyone during my campus tour? Other visitors? Friendly students? Potential roommates?

How clean is the campus? How noisy is the campus? Near an airport? Train tracks? Any strange scents/smells?

What type of clothes/fashion is worn? High priced? Comfy? Casual? More formal?

What about this campus makes me feel
comfortable? uncomfortable?

Do they have an Honors Program? What are the requirements?

How are the extracurricular activities?
Intramural sports? Drama? Music? Student
government?

Am I interested in official school teams? Sports?
Debate? What is the process to get more
information?

Are church services available? Religious clubs?
Bible studies? Off campus activities?

What type of counseling is available? Academic? Social?

How does Freshman Orientation work? How do you initially connect with people? Move-in process?

How do you register for classes? What is priority order?

How early in the day do classes start?
Night/Evening courses? Weekends?

Are there any foreign language requirements for all students? English requirements for foreign students?

What is the process to claim advanced credit?
Placement exams?

Are there opportunities to study abroad? To take mission trips?

Is there a diverse student body? What % of students are international/minorities? Are there specific diversity programs?

Do they offer any graduate degrees? Do high tech facilities cater to undergraduate or graduate students?

What is the student to professor ratio for my major? Student to teaching assistant ratios?

Is this primarily a commuter school? What percentage of student body leaves on the weekends?

How is the night life? Are there any curfews for students? Does this meet my expectations?

What restaurants are nearby? Local shopping? Coffee shops?

Is there a large fraternity or sorority presence on campus? Am I interested in this? Any specific organizations of interest?

What is the guy/girl ratio? Does this meet my expectations? Any campuses nearby with common activities?

Does this college have sports teams? How do students get tickets? Football? Basketball?

What is the weather like? Temperature ranges? Rain? Snow/ice?

What physical fitness activities are available?
Swimming? Gym? Trails? Tennis courts?

Is there a health clinic? Where do you go if you get sick or injured? Pharmacy nearby?

What allergies should I be concerned about in this climate? Do I have food allergies that need to be dealt with? How?

What do my parents think? Or someone else who I trust?

Does the college have any family events? Siblings day?

Who did I meet while on campus? Did I get their contact information?

What is the overall value of costs versus benefits of this college?

What is my feeling about selecting this college? Where does it fit on my priority list versus other colleges? Why?

Additional Thoughts

Additional Thoughts

Additional Thoughts

Additional Thoughts

What is the name of the college being
considered? Location? Public or private?
Website? Instagram? Facebook? Twitter?

What are my selection criteria? (Example: school size, costs, location) What is important in making my decision? My priorities?

How do I feel about the reputation of the school?
Nationally known? Top in region? Ranking for my
major?

What majors are available that I am interested in?

What is the placement rate for my major? What type of organizations are hiring?

How far away from home is this campus? Is the commute via car, train, bus, plane? Is this acceptable for me?

What is the average SAT/ACT score? Does my academic background fit?

What is the academic calendar? When does school start? end? Any fall breaks or long weekends? Holidays?

What are the costs for tuition? Room and board? Books and supplies?

What scholarships are available? Student loans? Work study?

Are part time jobs available on campus? Off campus? What are average hourly earning rates for students?

Is the college experiencing a budget deficit or surplus? Up-tick or down-tick in number of students? Large donations?

When did the most recent building renovation occur? Are there new facilities under construction? Building conditions?

How many students attend this college? Does it feel cramped or spacious?

How was the administrative staff? Did I feel welcome?

Is the college focused more on academics or more on developing you as a whole person? How can you determine?

What are methods for getting around campus?
Walk? Bike? Bus? Can a freshman have a car? Do
I need a car?

Did I feel safe on campus? Are there well lighted areas?

What is the surrounding community/area like?
High or low crime? Parks nearby? Urban area?
Museums?

How is the campus food? Are there a variety of food plans? Cafeteria? Food court?

What is the percentage of students from out-of-state? Anyone from my high school? Where are the students from?

How was the student center? Book store?
Common study areas?

How do I like the dorms? Did I see some cool dorm ideas? How many students to a room/suite? Visitation policy?

How is the technology on campus? WiFi everywhere? WiFi in dorms?

Did I meet any teachers? How did they make me feel?

Did I meet anyone during my campus tour? Other visitors? Friendly students? Potential roommates?

How clean is the campus? How noisy is the campus? Near an airport? Train tracks? Any strange scents/smells?

What type of clothes/fashion is worn? High priced? Comfy? Casual? More formal?

What about this campus makes me feel comfortable? uncomfortable?

Do they have an Honors Program? What are the requirements?

How are the extracurricular activities?
Intramural sports? Drama? Music? Student
government?

Am I interested in official school teams? Sports?
Debate? What is the process to get more
information?

Are church services available? Religious clubs?
Bible studies? Off campus activities?

What type of counseling is available? Academic?
Social?

How does Freshman Orientation work? How do you initially connect with people? Move-in process?

How do you register for classes? What is priority order?

How early in the day do classes start?
Night/Evening courses? Weekends?

Are there any foreign language requirements for all students? English requirements for foreign students?

What is the process to claim advanced credit?
Placement exams?

Are there opportunities to study abroad? To take mission trips?

Is there a diverse student body? What % of
students are international/minorities? Are there
specific diversity programs?

Do they offer any graduate degrees? Do high tech facilities cater to undergraduate or graduate students?

What is the student to professor ratio for my major? Student to teaching assistant ratios?

Is this primarily a commuter school? What percentage of student body leaves on the weekends?

How is the night life? Are there any curfews for students? Does this meet my expectations?

What restaurants are nearby? Local shopping? Coffee shops?

Is there a large fraternity or sorority presence on campus? Am I interested in this? Any specific organizations of interest?

What is the guy/girl ratio? Does this meet my expectations? Any campuses nearby with common activities?

Does this college have sports teams? How do students get tickets? Football? Basketball?

What is the weather like? Temperature ranges? Rain? Snow/ice?

What physical fitness activities are available?
Swimming? Gym? Trails? Tennis courts?

Is there a health clinic? Where do you go if you get sick or injured? Pharmacy nearby?

What allergies should I be concerned about in this climate? Do I have food allergies that need to be dealt with? How?

What do my parents think? Or someone else who I trust?

Does the college have any family events? Siblings day?

Who did I meet while on campus? Did I get their contact information?

What is the overall value of costs versus benefits of this college?

What is my feeling about selecting this college? Where does it fit on my priority list versus other colleges? Why?

Additional Thoughts

Additional Thoughts

Additional Thoughts

Additional Thoughts

Made in the USA
Monee, IL
09 May 2023